D1710894

Freedom
of Speech

Anna Maria Johnson

Cavendish
Square

New York

Published in 2020 by Cavendish Square Publishing, LLC
243 5th Avenue, Suite 136, New York, NY 10016

Library of Congress Cataloging-in-Publication Data

Names: Johnson, Anna Maria, author.
Title: Freedom of speech / Anna Maria Johnson.
Description: First edition. | New York : Cavendish Square, 2020. |
Series: Dilemmas in democracy | Includes bibliographical references and index. |
Audience: Grade 7 to 12.
Identifiers: LCCN 2018061293 (print) | LCCN 2019002322 (ebook) | ISBN 9781502645081 (ebook) |
ISBN 9781502645074 (library bound) | ISBN 9781502645067 (pbk.)
Subjects: LCSH: Freedom of speech--Juvenile literature. |
Freedom of speech--United States--Juvenile literature.
Classification: LCC JC591 (ebook) | LCC JC591 .J63 2020 (print) | DDC 323.44/30973--dc23
LC record available at https://lccn.loc.gov/2018061293

Editorial Director: David McNamara
Editor: Caitlyn Miller
Copy Editor: Alex Tessman
Associate Art Director: Alan Sliwinski
Designer: Christina Shults
Production Coordinator: Karol Szymczuk
Photo Research: J8 Media

The photographs in this book are used by permission and through the courtesy of:
Cover Tony Tallec/Alamy Stock Photo; background (and used throughout the book) Artist Elizaveta/
Shutterstock.com; p. 4 Jack R Perry Photography/Shutterstock.com; p. 9 Education Images/
Universal Images Group/Getty Images; p. 10 Freedomz/Shutterstock.com; p. 15 SOPA Images/
LightRocket/Getty Images; p. 19 Hero Images/Getty Images; p. 20 Fotosearch/Archive Photos/
Getty Images; p. 24 Bloomberg/Getty Images; p. 27 RoSonic/Shutterstock.com; p. 28 Mike Peel/
Wikimedia Commons/ File:First amendment engraving,Washington DC.jpg/CC-BY-SA-4.0;
pp. 34-45 Boston Globe/Getty Images; p. 42 NurPhoto/Getty Images; p. 45 Album/Alamy Stock
Photo; p. 47 ©AP Images; p. 48 Scott J. Ferrell/CQ-Roll Call Group/Getty Images; p. 51 PHAS/
Universal Images Group/Getty Images; p. 53 sdecoret/Shutterstock.com; p. 55 Maina Kiai/Wikimedia
Commons/File:UN Special Rapporteur David Kaye (freedom of opinion all sizes and expression)
speaks during the June 16 side event "Religion Use this file Meets Rights" organized by FORUMA
on the SIA(cropped).jpg/CC-BY-SA-2.0; p. 56 Joseph Sohm/Shutterstock.com; pp. 58-59 a katz/
Shutterstock.com; p. 62 Michael Zagaris/Getty Images; p. 65 Diego G Diaz/Shutterstock.com; p. 66
Mark Ralston/AFP/Getty Images; p. 68 Leigh Vogel/Getty Images; p. 71 CharityNavigator.org.

Printed in the United States of America

CONTENTS

Congress OF THE United States

begun and held at the City of New-York, on
Wednesday the fourth of March, one thousand seven hundred and eighty nine

THE Conventions of a number of the States, having at the time of their adopting the Constitution, expressed a desire, in order to prevent misconstruction or abuse of its powers, that further declaratory and restrictive clauses should be added: And as extending the ground of public confidence in the Government, will best ensure the beneficent ends of its institution.

RESOLVED by the Senate and House of Representatives of the United States of America, in Congress assembled, two thirds of both Houses concurring, that the following Articles be proposed to the Legislatures of the several States, as amendments to the Constitution of the United States, all, or any of which Articles, when ratified by three fourths of the said Legislatures, to be valid to all intents and purposes, as part of the said Constitution, viz.

ARTICLES in addition to, and Amendment of the Constitution of the United States of America, proposed by Congress, and ratified by the Legislatures of the several States, pursuant to the fifth Article of the original Constitution.

the first ... After the first enumeration required by the first Article of the Constitution, there shall be one Representative for every thirty thousand, until the number shall amount to one hundred, after which the proportion shall be so regulated by Congress, that there shall be not less than one hundred Representatives, nor less than one Representative for every forty thousand persons, until the number of Representatives shall amount to two hundred, after which the proportion shall be so regulated by Congress, that there shall not be less than two hundred Representatives, nor more than one Representative for every fifty thousand persons.

the second ... No law, varying the compensation for the services of the Senators and Representatives, shall take effect, until an election of Representatives shall have intervened.

the third ... Congress shall make no law respecting an establishment of religion, or prohibiting the free exercise thereof; or abridging the freedom of speech, or of the press; or the right of the people peaceably to assemble, and to petition the Government for a redress of grievances.

the fourth ... A well regulated militia, being necessary to the security of a free State, the right of the people to keep and bear Arms, shall not be infringed.

the fifth ... No Soldier shall, in time of peace be quartered in any house, without the consent of the Owner, nor in time of war, but in a manner to be prescribed by law.

the sixth ... The right of the people to be secure in their persons, houses, papers, and effects, against unreasonable searches and seizures, shall not be violated, and no Warrants shall issue, but upon probable cause, supported by Oath or affirmation, and particularly describing the place to be searched, and the persons or things to be seized.

the seventh ... No person shall be held to answer for a capital, or otherwise infamous crime, unless on a presentment or indictment of a Grand Jury, except in cases arising in the land or naval forces, or in the Militia, when in actual service in time of War or public danger; nor shall any person be subject for the same offence to be twice put in jeopardy of life or limb; nor shall be compelled in any criminal case to be a witness against himself, nor be deprived of life, liberty, or property, without due process of law; nor shall private property be taken for public use without just compensation.

the eighth ... In all criminal prosecutions, the accused shall enjoy the right to a speedy and public trial, by an impartial jury of the State and district wherein the crime shall have been committed, which district shall have been previously ascertained by law, and to be informed of the nature and cause of the accusation; to be confronted with the witnesses against him; to have compulsory process for obtaining witnesses in his favor, and to have the Assistance of Counsel for his defence.

the ninth ... In suits at common law, where the value in controversy shall exceed twenty dollars, the right of trial by jury shall be preserved, and no fact tried by a jury, shall be otherwise re-examined in any Court of the United States, than according to the rules of the common law.

the tenth ... Excessive bail shall not be required, nor excessive fines imposed, nor cruel and unusual punishments inflicted.

the eleventh ... The enumeration in the Constitution, of certain rights, shall not be construed to deny or disparage others retained by the people.

the twelfth ... The powers not delegated to the United States by the Constitution, nor prohibited by it to the States, are reserved to the States respectively, or to the people.

ATTEST,

Frederick Augustus Muhlenberg, Speaker of the House of Representatives.

John Adams, Vice President of the United States, and President of the

John Beckley, Clerk of the House of Representatives.

Sam. A. Otis Secretary of the Senate.

CHAPTER 1

What Is Freedom of Speech?

Before the United States Constitution was ratified, the Founding Fathers debated for months about what rights should be included. Some believed that anything that wasn't mentioned in the Constitution would be left to the state governments. Others believed that certain rights should be stated as a guarantee of protection for Americans. They worried that if rights were not written down, people might not have them in the future. Thomas Jefferson told James Madison, "Half a loaf is better than no bread. If we cannot secure all rights, let us secure what we can."

As a result of this conversation, ten amendments, together called the Bill of Rights, were added to the Constitution in 1791. The First Amendment grants Americans five specific freedoms, including the freedom of speech. Free speech is closely related to the freedom of religion and religious expression. It also relates to freedom of the press, which means the right to publish information for the public to read. The

Opposite: The Bill of Rights consists of ten amendments to the US Constitution. Freedom of speech is part of the First Amendment.

rights to peacefully assemble and to ask the government to make changes to policy have been interpreted to allow nonviolent protests of all types within the nation. The First Amendment says:

> *Congress shall make no law respecting an establishment of religion, or prohibiting the free exercise thereof; or abridging the freedom of speech, or of the press; or the right of the people peaceably to assemble, and to petition the Government for a redress of grievances.*

In other words, the federal (national) government may not choose for its citizens which religion they must believe or practice. The federal government must allow its people to speak their minds without fear of punishment, and the press must be able to write and publish freely—even when they're critical of the government. Finally, people must not be limited from gathering together and asking their government for changes.

These five rights—the freedom of religion, freedom of speech, freedom of the press, the right to assembly, and the right to protest—are the foundations of American democracy. The First Amendment has also inspired similar protections in other democracies throughout the world. The 1942 Universal Declaration of Human Rights borrows from this language as well. This document was created after World War II by people who believed that all human beings should have certain rights. It was designed to be something like a Bill of Rights for all people.

Across the board, freedom of speech and freedom of expression are highly valued in democracies. Without such freedoms, governments could refuse to listen to people who voice concerns or criticisms about injustice and unfair laws. In countries without freedom of speech, citizens must be careful never to criticize or complain in public about their government because they could risk going to jail for doing so. Since a democracy is based on the idea of government by the people, freedom of speech is essential. It allows citizens to participate fully in the process of government.

Censorship

The opposite of freedom of speech is censorship. Censorship is when news, books, films, or other sources of information are removed or withheld, in full or in part, by an authority figure. Censorship occurs when authorities decide something is obscene, unacceptable for political reasons, or a threat to security. Censorship can occur on many levels ranging from the federal government, to state and local governments, local school districts, and even on specific digital platforms and sites.

One common example of censorship is when certain books are banned from libraries or from a school curriculum. People from different political views have wished to censor books for different reasons. For example, some books have been banned for being too violent or sexually explicit. Other books have been banned for using offensive or racist language.

During a time of war, governments might censor some information in order to protect national security. Historically, this has often led to controversies or mistrust when people later found out that vital information was kept secret.

Starting in 1982, the American Library Association has celebrated "Banned Books Week" each year in September. Librarians, bookstores, teachers, and readers share their support for the freedom to read and express ideas.

Regulating Free Speech

It is important to note that there is a difference between censorship (which is often seen as negative) and normal regulations that are needed in order to promote safety and the functioning of a healthy democracy.

In the United States, the First Amendment has been interpreted by the courts during the past century to generally increase protections. American citizens have the ability to express their opinions and ideas even when those ideas are critical of the government. However, freedom of speech is not absolute. Over time, some limitations have been defined too. These limitations have usually been determined as the result of court cases. The Supreme Court has ruled that certain kinds of harmful speech are not allowed.

Clear and Present Danger

In 1919, in the case of *Schenk v. United States*, the Supreme Court stated that even "the most stringent protection of free speech would not protect a man in falsely shouting fire in a theatre and causing panic … The question in every case is whether the words used are used in such circumstances and are of such a nature as to create a clear and present danger." Simply put, words that cause a "clear and present danger" are not protected by the First Amendment. If a person were to shout "Fire!" in a crowd when there was not a real fire, this could create a dangerous situation, such as a stampede. Yelling "Fire!" would be taking the principle of freedom of speech too far. Under such circumstances, protecting safety takes priority. Today, this is known as the "clear and present danger test."

Fighting Words

Later, in 1942, another Supreme Court case used similar logic to draw another boundary. The *Chaplinsky v. New Hampshire* case established that "fighting words" could be restricted without violating the First Amendment. "Fighting words" include language that is insulting, harmful, and intended to provoke violence.

Again, the court determined that freedom of speech does not extend to harming others, and that the government or state may sometimes use its power to suppress harmful speech to maintain order. It can be difficult to define what "fighting words" are, so use of this particular limitation is rare.

A Supreme Court ruling in 1969, *Brandenburg v. Ohio*, created a test to limit the punishment of speech that encourages violence.

A set of scales is often used as a symbol of justice because justice requires balancing the rights and responsibilities of different parties.

Obscenity and the Miller Test

The Supreme Court has ruled that making or distributing obscene materials is not protected by the First Amendment. In 1957, the case of *Roth v. United States* made this clear with a ruling that upheld a California law against sending obscene books through the mail. Obscenity laws highlight a major dilemma surrounding free speech. Courts have struggled with how to define "obscenity" for a very long time.

Since 1973, courts have used the "Miller test" to decide whether something is obscene. The Miller test has three parts: (1) the average person, using present-day common standards, would agree that the work is obscene, (2) the work describes, in an offensive way, sexual conduct prohibited by state law, and (3) the work "lacks literary, artistic, political, or scientific value." This test was established by Supreme Court in the case of *Miller v. California*.

The definition of what is considered "obscene" has changed over time, but still there are certain types of content that is not legally permitted to be created or shared. The rules about obscenity are stricter when minors are involved than the rules for adults. For example, it is not permitted for people to send or post nude pictures on the internet if they will be seen by people under the age of eighteen.

Other Limitations to Freedom of Speech

Although freedom of speech is well-protected at the federal level, additional limits apply in certain circumstances. The US Courts web page "What Does Free Speech Mean?" gives examples. For instance, the Supreme Court has ruled that students in public school may not

The Brandenburg Test

In 1969, a leader of the Ku Klux Klan (KKK) named Clarence Brandenburg gave a speech at a rally in which he and others used racial slurs against African Americans and Jews. He said, "it's possible that there might have to be some revengeance [sic] taken." Video footage by an Ohio reporter showed twelve people burning a cross and wearing white hooded robes. Speeches criticized the president, Congress, and the Supreme Court. The state of Ohio then convicted Brandenburg of violating an Ohio state law.

This case led to the Supreme Court decision of *Brandenburg v. Ohio*. The court created a test to determine when the state government may be allowed to restrict speech that encourages violence or crime. The test includes two parts: (1) the speech in question is "directed to inciting or producing imminent lawless action," and (2) the speech is "likely to incite or produce such action." In other words, when a person gives a speech that encourages others to be violent, the state government might enforce limits in certain situations. But this is rare. The government would need to prove that the speech could likely lead to real danger and is not just talk. Since Brandenburg's audience was judged to be "unlikely" to follow through with violence (part 2 of the test), and in fact did not, the court ruled in Brandenburg's favor.

The Brandenburg Test has been used in more recent cases. In 1982, civil rights activist Charles Evers threatened violence against people who refused to boycott white businesses. The National Association for the Advancement of Colored People (NAACP) took Evers's side against Claiborne Hardware Company. In their ruling on *NAACP v. Claiborne Hardware Co.*, the court decided that Evers's speech was protected just as Brandenburg's had been. Since Evers' speech did not actually cause lawless action, it was deemed "protected."

print material in school newspapers without permission of their teachers and administration. Students cannot "make an obscene speech at a school-sponsored event." Students cannot promote the use of illegal drugs in school.

Freedom of Speech in the Workplace

Like schools, workplaces may also place conditions and limits on employees' speech based on what is considered appropriate within the company. Employees may be fired from their jobs for violating such rules. According to the professional legal organization FindLaw, freedom of speech within the workplace depends on several factors including whether the workplace is public or private, what type of speech is involved, and the employee's position.

Aside from the First Amendment, other laws may provide a degree of protection to employees, however. Antidiscrimination laws and various local laws may protect certain kinds of employee speech. Some states have laws against discriminating against employees for belonging to political groups.

Extremist and Hate Speech

Due to court decisions, the United States has one of the most tolerant views of extremist and hate speech of any democracy. Because it is hard to prove a direct cause and effect relationship between hate speech and violent actions, hate speech in the United States goes largely unchecked. Other democracies view the United States as being excessively tolerant of speech that elsewhere is banned for being hateful, violent, or extremist. In recent years, Americans' hate and extremist speech online has had real-life consequences both in the United States and abroad.

In the United States, hate crimes have been rising since 2015. According to the Federal Bureau of Investigation (FBI), a hate crime is defined as a "criminal offense against a person or property motivated in whole or in part by an offender's bias against a race, religion, disability, sexual orientation, ethnicity, gender, or gender identity."

According to the FBI's annual report, hate crimes rose 17 percent in 2017. There were 7,175 so-called bias crimes, which targeted 8,493 victims based on race and sexual orientation. It was the third year in a row that hate crimes rose, and the rise was at a substantially higher rate than the previous two years. By comparison, 2016 saw 6,121 hate crimes, 2015 saw 5,858, and 2014 saw 5,479 hate crimes. About 59.6 percent of hate crimes in 2017 were based on race, 20.6 percent were based on religion, and 15.8 percent were based on sexual orientation.

Some people believe that the rise of hate crimes is the result of greater opportunities to share and spread hate speech through new media, such as websites, blogs, social media, and YouTube.

On the other hand, when speech is suppressed, great harm can occur. When governments limit the freedom of speech or freedom of the press, this can dampen democracy, which is based on full participation by all citizens. Within the United States, the right to peacefully protest is considered part of freedom of speech. American citizens commonly gather to protest policies with which they disagree or which they believe violate important values of being an American. When protests are shut down, society loses the chance to debate the topic and hear all sides and perspectives.

After a deadly shooting at the Tree of Life synagogue in Pittsburgh, Pennsylvania, thousands of people gathered to honor the victims and share the message that their community was "stronger than hate."

Theories of Free Speech

Over time, different theories have been developed to support unrestricted free speech in the United States. The marketplace of ideas theory is the best known. More recently, other theories have been added: the democratic theory, the tolerant society theory, the individual autonomy theory, and the checking value theory.

In 1919, US Supreme Court justice Oliver Wendell Holmes wrote that freedom of speech was similar to a free economy. He described a "marketplace of ideas" in which all ideas could be expressed, no matter their quality. He believed that the best ideas would become more popular and successful, while bad ideas would fall by the wayside over time. He thought that as long as everyone was allowed to speak freely, people could hear all the options and choose the best ones.

In 1948, just after World War II had ended, Alexander Meiklejohn developed a different theory to support freedom of speech. He thought that free speech was important for a democratic form of government because democracy is, essentially, a government formed by the people's opinions and discussions. The Constitution includes the idea that the government was formed by the people and for the people. According to Meiklejohn, therefore, all words should be listened to as part of public discussion and debate. This theory is also sometimes called the "self-government free speech theory."

Later, a professor named Lee Bollinger developed a third theory to support freedom of speech. He thought that listening to all ideas, even bad ones, helps to promote self-restraint, self-discipline, and tolerance for differences. By listening to other ideas different from one's own, one learns to become a better, more tolerant person. Bollinger developed this theory in his 1986 book, *The Tolerant Society: Freedom of Speech and Extremist Speech in America*.

Yet another theory related to freedom of speech is the individual autonomy theory, which states simply that every individual has the right to have opinions and to express them. The checking value theory relates primarily to the role of the press. In a democracy, the press plays an important role as "watchdog of the government." A free press is vital to a free society because it ensures that the public is well-informed of facts and policies. A free press can criticize government policies, actions, and leaders without fear of punishment, providing accountability.

Justifications for Freedom of Speech

The theories in support of free speech are built on a foundation of four key reasons why freedom of speech is so important in a democracy. In short, these four reasons, or justifications, include: democracy, the social contract, the pursuit of the truth, and individual autonomy. These four justifications have been used to explain why American free speech laws go so far as to protect even hate, extremist, and defamatory speech.

The first justification for free speech is that Americans live in a democracy. A democracy is, by definition, the rule of the people, by the people, for the people. Therefore, the people must be free to express their ideas, opinions, and beliefs in order to support the ideal of a democratic form of government.

The second justification is the idea of a "social contract." The United States was formed during the Enlightenment, an important movement in history when people thought about and wrote many books about how government and people should behave. The famous Enlightenment writer John Locke wrote about the idea of a "social contract." Locke wrote that human beings willingly give up a small portion of their personal rights in order to gain protection from an acceptable form of government. This deal is like a contract that people make with their government. The "social contract" idea influenced Thomas Jefferson, who helped to found

Scholar Lee Bollinger says that all speech is valuable, even bad ideas. He argues that listening to others' ideas promotes self-restraint, self-discipline, and tolerance for differences.

the United States, and in turn, James Madison, who wrote much of the text of the Constitution and the Bill of Rights.

The third justification is that people have the right to pursue the truth. One important reason why people should be able to express their ideas freely is to find the truth. By hearing different viewpoints and thinking about them rationally and logically, a person is more likely to discover the truth. This theory assumes that people are rational and will be able to recognize the truth when they hear it.

The fourth justification has to do with individual autonomy. It is based on the idea that every human being (individual) has inherent worth and the right to express himself or herself. Freedom of expression is therefore closely linked to the dignity of each person and is therefore a human right.

How Freedom of Speech Has Evolved

As times have changed, so have the means by which people communicate their ideas. In light of new communication platforms such as blogs and social media, freedom of speech and its boundaries change to keep up. Older laws address forms of speech in print or spoken in public. However, a post on social media is a little different from either of these. Recent debates ask whether a tweet or Snapchat post should be held to the same standard as an article printed in a newspaper. When people use social media, they don't always think about what they write as a permanent document. Yet their words can live on digitally, even after the person who wrote a post deletes it. Therefore, it can be unclear how to apply current libel or slander laws to online contexts.

From its infancy, the United States has discussed the importance of freedom of speech, and the conversation has continued through the centuries. Each generation has re-interpreted the First

Amendment and redrawn its boundaries to suit new cultural and historical contexts. Founding Fathers such as Thomas Jefferson, George Mason, and James Madison exchanged letters in which they warned of the dangers of too many limits being placed on individuals and on the press. They all agreed this freedom was important, even though they had different ideas about the best way to protect it. During the twentieth century, local, state, and federal courts have looked carefully at different forms of expression as it has played out in culture. Sometimes the courts have ruled on the side of greater freedom, while other times they have ruled on the side of other values like safety or community expectations. Over the years, scholars and ordinary citizens have explored different ways to explain why it is good for society when people are able to express themselves freely.

Today, courts must grapple with cases relating to freedom of speech and social media sites, blogs, and other internet publications.

The Universal Declaration of Human Rights

Eleanor Roosevelt holds a large copy of the Universal Declaration of Human Rights in 1947.

In 1945, not long after World War II had ended, the United Nations (UN) was formed to bring peace to the world. Eleanor Roosevelt, the Chair of the UN Human Rights Commission and wife of American president Franklin D. Roosevelt, created a document intended to guarantee basic human rights for all people, recognizing their dignity.

This document that protects freedom of speech and many other rights is similar to the Bill of Rights in the United States Constitution and the Declaration of the Rights of Man (from the French Revolution, 1789). As of 2018, 192 countries have signed on to the Universal Declaration of Human Rights.

This document declares many rights for human beings, but the parts that are most similar to the United States First Amendment are articles 18 through 20:

Article 18.
Everyone has the right to freedom of thought, conscience and religion; this right includes freedom to change his religion or belief, and freedom, either alone or in community with others and in public or private,

to manifest his religion or belief in teaching, practice, worship, and observance.

Article 19.
Everyone has the right to freedom of opinion and expression; this right includes freedom to hold opinions without interference and to seek, receive and impart information and ideas through any media and regardless of frontiers.

Article 20.
1. *Everyone has the right to freedom of peaceful assembly and association.*
2. *No one may be compelled to belong to an association.*

The above articles clearly guarantee freedom of expression in various forms, but unlike the US Constitution, the international document also specifies that there may be some limitations. Article 29 states there may be limitations "as determined by law solely for the purpose of securing due recognition and respect for the rights and freedoms of others and of meeting the just requirements of morality, public order, and the general welfare in a democratic society." In other words, each person may have rights but only to the extent that the rights and safety of others are also protected.

As a result of Article 29, the international community, including many democracies as well as countries with different forms of government, has been more willing to accept laws that draw some boundaries on freedom of expression. In contrast, since the US Constitution does not state clear limitations, it has been left up to the courts to determine when limiting rights may be appropriate.

CHAPTER 2

Freedom of Speech in America Today

Nearly every week, a story appears in the news about threats to American citizens' freedom of speech. At the other end of the spectrum are stories about the problems caused by people expressing their views in ways that inconvenience or trouble others. One news story from 2018 involved a prominent radio talk host responsible for spreading false information and conspiracy theories. That year, other stories relating to free speech focused on social issues like police shootings of unarmed African American men, sexual harassment and violence, student protests of current gun laws, and immigration.

In 2018, there were a record number of protests responding to important issues like climate change, women's rights, immigrant children being separated from their parents at the Mexican-American border, and more. Each movement and

Opposite: Protesters in San Diego express their opposition to President Trump's proposed border wall in March 2018.

protest sparked lively conversations about what ways are appropriate to express an opinion and where lines should be drawn.

In the present day, we often look to the past to see where lines were drawn before and what consequences followed. Yet the world we live in is quite different than it was thirty or forty years ago. In light of the globally-connected world, we need to revisit our understandings and assumptions of what freedom of expression looks like and how our interpretations need to evolve and be developed.

Common Misconceptions

Freedom of speech, and its limitations, are commonly misunderstood since the First Amendment technically states only that the government may not limit the people's freedom of expression. Many other sectors of society, however, can legally limit what people under their authority may say without violating the Constitution. Private employers, school boards and administrators, state and local governments, and parents have the authority to make rules and set boundaries around speech and expression. For example, schools may set dress codes and rules about what type of language is permitted on campus. Most teens are well aware that parents establish house rules limiting the ways their children may express themselves! Similarly, employers usually have rules guiding the behavior and speech of their employees. Workers who break the rules can be reprimanded or even fired from their jobs.

Looking beyond the law, freedom of speech is an important cultural symbol. People often confuse the legal definition (matters of law) with the cultural value of free speech (social conventions). Therefore, when employees, public figures, or athletes express free speech in unexpected ways, the public may struggle to determine whether such speech should be defended.

Current Debates About Social Media Companies

The most significant recent development in freedom of speech is the rise of the internet as an important means of communicating ideas. Thanks to social media platforms like Facebook, Twitter, Snapchat, and Instagram, people can share ideas more quickly and widely than ever before.

While television and radio have special rules that govern what can be said or shown, there are no formal bodies overseeing what happens in online speech. There is widespread public debate about whether the government should get more involved in deciding what is permitted online. However, it is difficult for the government to moderate online speech without violating the protections of the First Amendment.

In 1997, the Supreme Court struck down part of a federal law called the Communications Decency Act because they thought it would interfere with the "free exchange of ideas" in the "marketplace of ideas." Instead, Facebook, Twitter, Google, and other major media companies regulate themselves. Therefore, they play a powerful role in promoting and limiting speech. For example, Facebook and Twitter users must follow the rules set up in the user agreement or their account can be blocked or suspended. Each platform sets its own definitions for hate and extremist speech, abusive behavior, and the like.

Facebook, for example, doesn't allow "nudity or other sexually suggestive content; hate speech, credible threats or direct attacks on

The First Amendment to the Constitution is engraved on the Newseum in Washington, DC.

Thomas Jefferson was concerned that the original United States Constitution did not offer enough guarantees of rights for individuals in the new country. On December 20, 1787, Jefferson wrote a letter to its author, James Madison, about what he liked and did not like in the proposed Constitution. In part, Jefferson said:

> *I will now add what I do not like. First the omission of a bill of rights providing clearly and without the aid of sophisms for freedom of religion, freedom of the press, protection against standing armies, restriction against monopolies ... Let me add that a bill of rights is what the people are entitled to against every government on earth, general or particular, and what no just government should refuse, or rest on inference.*

By 1789, he persuaded James Madison to add the amendments that are today known as the Bill of Rights to the founding document. Since then, the First Amendment has become one of the most celebrated parts of the Constitution.

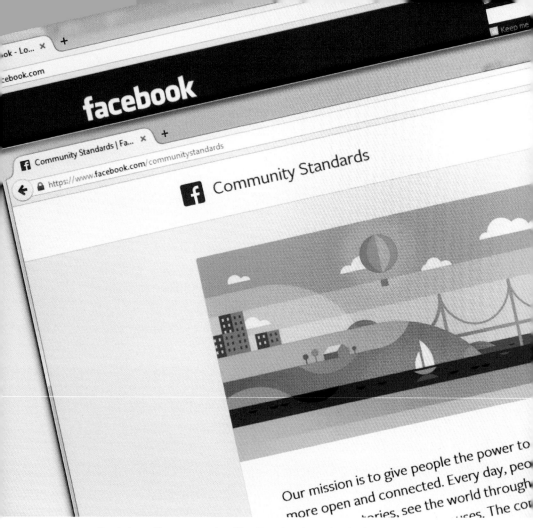

Social media companies like Facebook make their own rules about what kinds of speech are allowed on their platforms.

an individual or group; content that contains self-harm or excessive violence; fake or imposter profiles; spam." It also allows its users to report any posts that violate the Facebook Community Standards. According to the Community Standards, Facebook's mission is "all about embracing diverse views." Facebook's mission continues by saying,

We err on the side of allowing content, even when some find it objectionable, unless removing that content can prevent a specific harm. Moreover, at times we will allow content that might otherwise violate our standards if we feel that it is newsworthy, significant, or important to the public interest. We do this only after weighing the public interest value of the content against the risk of real-world harm.

Similarly, "The Twitter Rules" state that "everyone should have the power to create and share ideas and information instantly, without barriers. In order to protect the experience and safety of people who use Twitter, there are some limitations on the type of content and behavior that we allow." If users don't follow the Twitter Rules, their accounts can be suspended temporarily or permanently.

Content that is not allowed on Twitter includes copyrighted material (without permission), graphic violence including pictures of surgery, and pictures of people who have died (if their family has requested that these images be removed). Threats of violence, harm to others, suicide, and self-harm are also not allowed on Twitter. Sharing other people's private information is a violation too. Fake accounts, spam, and inflating an account's number of followers are all forbidden activities, according to the Twitter Rules.

A Closer Look at Social Media and Free Speech: The Case of Alex Jones

In 2012, a school shooting in Sandy Hook, Connecticut, resulted in the deaths of twenty-six people, twenty of whom were elementary school children. Soon after the news broke, a far-right radio host named Alex Jones began to make claims that the shooting had been staged, or faked. He repeated this conspiracy theory on his radio show InfoWars and shared videos about it on YouTube, gaining millions of followers. The videos claimed that the parents who had lost their children were actors participating in a hoax. Listeners of the show believed Jones and began to harass the parents in Sandy Hook, even making death threats. This harassment continued for five years, with Jones continuing to make false statements on his show and on social media about the parents and children of Sandy Hook. Each year on the anniversary of the massacre, some of Jones's listeners even travel to Sandy Hook to protest and threaten the parents and survivors. One family has moved seven times to escape harassment.

Finally, in spring 2018, some of the parents of children who were killed filed a lawsuit against Alex Jones. Five lawsuits were filed against Jones for defamation, which includes libel and slander. According to the Media Law Resource Center, libel includes false statements made about a person "in written or other permanent form." Slander includes false statements made about a person in "verbal statements or gestures." "Defamatory" means that the statement caused actual harm to a person's reputation, not that it was merely offensive or insulting.

Jones then countersued, claiming First Amendment protections of free speech. By this time, he had admitted that the shooting was not a hoax, but Jones claimed he had the right to invent stories and share them. A judge rejected Mr. Jones's argument in one case. According to BBC News, a case like this is important because "in an era of fake news and social media, this suit may have an impact on future free speech claims, especially those concerning social media figures."

Although the five defamation cases against Alex Jones are still in process, they have had some impact already—but not when it comes to the government regulation. Instead, Jones's speech has been regulated by private social medial companies. Social media platforms including Apple, YouTube, Facebook, and Spotify deleted some Infowars content from their sites in August 2018, citing hate speech. In September 2018, Twitter said it permanently suspended the accounts of Alex Jones and his InfoWars website after several tweets that violated Twitter's abusive behavior policy.

The legal cases involving Alex Jones raise questions for the American public about how much power private companies should have to regulate what people can post on the internet. Is it best to leave the government out of regulating online speech, which is the current practice? Or should social media companies be regulated in what they can permit or limit? Do we want Google, Twitter, and Facebook to make decisions about what speech is permitted to be freely expressed, and what should be banned?

Current Debates About Free Speech in Schools

In recent years, educators and administrators have struggled with the question of how to best allow their students to freely express themselves while also maintaining a safe and orderly environment where students can learn.

Students have the constitutionally protected right to free speech at school. In 1969, the US Supreme Court ruled in favor of students who had been suspended from school for wearing black armbands in protest of the US war in Vietnam. The court ruled in *Tinker v. Des Moines Independent Community School District* that schools may not regulate student speech unless it "materially disrupts classwork or involves substantial disorder or invasion of the rights of others."

At 10:00 a.m. on April 20, 2018, American students around the country took action during the school day to protest gun violence in their schools. They called it National School Walkout Day. Different school districts responded in different ways to students' political expression.

Since 1969, various courts have ruled that schools can regulate student speech that "materially disrupts the school setting or interferes with the rights of others; is lewd, vulgar, or obscene" on the ground that such speech "undermines the school's basic educational mission." It has also ruled in favor of regulating school-sponsored speech, as long as those limits are reasonably related to legitimate teaching concerns or are related to speech that promotes activities that are illegal, such as illegal drug use.

In 2018, the National School Board Association released a new publication called "Coercion, Conscience, and the First Amendment: A Legal Guide for Public Schools on the Regulation of Student and Employee Speech." It offers guidance about appropriate actions in schools when a student athlete takes a knee during the national anthem or when students organize a national protest to ask for a change in gun laws.

The publication provides an example from a recent issue in public schools. In San Pasqual Valley Unified School District, a federal district court ruled on the side of a varsity football player who knelt during the National Anthem as part of a nationwide movement protesting racial injustice. Different school districts have responded in different ways to students "taking a knee" as a form of protest.

Current Debates About Free Speech in Workplaces

Government employees have more protections for free speech than those who work for private companies. Private employers may make rules about what is acceptable for employees to say or write/post in public spaces. According to Comply Right, speech that is not allowed in workplaces includes sharing confidential information, controversial political views, rude jokes or comments, and profanity. Recently, government employees have also been restricted in what they may post on social media about political topics.

On the other hand, the National Labor Relations Act (NLRA), passed in 1935, allows employees to talk about their working conditions and share salary information. Employers have the responsibility of preventing harassment and discrimination among their employees. They cannot allow offensive comments about race, gender, religion, age, or sexual orientation. Even comments that an employee makes on social media can count. An employer can take action to prevent a hostile workplace environment for other workers.

Business Insider magazine reported on one employee of Google who caught national attention in August 2017 when he sent a ten-page memo to people in his workplace. In it, he wrote that biological differences make women less suited to working in the tech industry. His employer, Google CEO Sundar Pichai, responded:

> *First, let me say that we strongly support the right of Googlers to express themselves, and much of what was in that memo is fair to debate, regardless of whether a vast majority of Googlers disagree with it. However, portions of the memo violate our Code of Conduct and cross the line by advancing harmful gender stereotypes in our workplace … To suggest a group of our colleagues have traits that make them less biologically suited to that work is offensive and not OK.*

The employee who wrote the memo was fired from his job.

Media Bias

Whenever a news story breaks about freedom of speech, such as the example of the Google employee above, different versions of the story appear in different sources. Some sources emphasized the point of view of the employee and his right to his opinion. Others emphasized the company's responsibility to maintain a safe and comfortable work environment for all employees.

Different news sources may cover the same event in different ways depending on their viewpoint and mission. Critical thinkers make a habit of reading different news sources in order to hear a balanced view rather than trusting only one source.

Different sources may use headlines and tone to present a particular view or stance on protests. For example, a Google search for "NFL anthem protests" will reveal many different headlines, some with a positive tone and others with a negative one. Usually, a headline that sticks to the facts and avoids sounding inflammatory will indicate a more reliable and trustworthy source of information.

Many organizations try to help readers sort out which sources of information are politically biased and which are more neutral. There can also be a range in terms of sticking to facts versus including opinion and interpretation. It is a good idea to start with news sources that focus on the facts: who, what, when, where, why, and how. Only after the facts are established, a critical reader might then read additional sources that include commentary, analysis, and opinion. If an opinion or analysis seems to slant to a particular side, skilled readers will try to find another source with a different viewpoint to avoid taking a one-sided approach to news.

Attorney Vanessa Otero has founded an organization that works to identify political bias in popular news sources and which encourages readers to read across the spectrum to get a "balanced diet." She compares reading habits to eating habits, saying it is important to hear a variety of viewpoints just as it is important to eat a variety of foods. It is worth mentioning that some news sources are like "junk food." It is best to limit or avoid junk sources that make no attempt to provide good quality journalism.

The Paradox of Tolerance

Complicated situations relating to free speech raise an important question: If someone shares views that put down the value of other people, what is the appropriate response?

What is the appropriate way for a tolerant person to respond to intolerance? Should the tolerant person call out or even ban intolerance for the sake of promoting tolerance? Or should the tolerant person be willing to tolerate even ideas that are offensive or hateful to him or her? These questions relate to "the paradox of tolerance," which has been answered in different ways. Some scholars have concluded that tolerating intolerance will eventually lead to an increasingly intolerant society because hateful or extremist speech and ideas are left to flourish and grow. An example of this viewpoint is from Karl Popper's book *The Open Society and its Enemies*, which names this paradox.

Other scholars think that a truly tolerant society will be strong and mature enough to listen to even offensive speech because it can make us more self-disciplined and confident. This contrasting view was developed by professor Lee Bollinger, president of Columbia University.

To complicate the matter, American history offers us examples of the risks of both scenarios. Each approach has its own costs, benefits, and dangers. On one hand, tolerating hate speech has sometimes led to violence. A recent example from American history is Dylann Roof, an avowed white supremacist, who entered an African American church on June 17, 2015, and killed nine people. National Public Radio's The Two-Way reported that Roof "told investigators that his beliefs about race were shaped by things he read on the internet after an initial Google search for information about Trayvon Martin, the unarmed black teenager shot and killed in 2012." For Dylann Roof, reading racist online material helped to shape his viewpoint and seems to have helped lead him to the decision to kill. Violent actions often start with violent talk. Of course, many people who make racist or hateful comments do not go on to commit violence. Therefore, it is important to ask where lines should be drawn.

Popper wrote that tolerance of intolerance would lead to more intolerance. Bollinger concluded the opposite—that tolerance of intolerance would, in turn, lead to greater tolerance. Both offer valuable questions for any democratic society to ask, but they come to different conclusions. This conversation is sure to continue for a long time without finding clear answers. One thing is certain, however. Freedom of speech is not absolute. It must be balanced with other important values and considerations. The question is a matter of how much weight to place on each side of the scale.

When Hate Speech Turns into Violence

On October 27, 2018, Robert D. Bowers opened fire in a Pittsburgh Jewish synagogue, Tree of Life, while shouting anti-Semitic slurs. He killed eleven worshippers and one police officer, wounding others. The *New York Times* reported that Bowers had spent the previous months posting racist comments and memes online, calling Jews the "enemy of white people" and "children of Satan." Bowers used a social networking app called Gab, which calls itself a "free speech alternative" to Facebook and Twitter because Gab had almost no restrictions on what users could post. Gab allowed Bowers to connect with other alt-right activists, white nationalists, and Nazis.

A social media app cannot run on its own. It depends on a domain name provider like GoDaddy, a payment processing platform such as PayPal, and a web hosting service. After news broke that the Tree of Life shooter was connected to Gab, Gab's service providers cut ties with Gab, taking it temporarily offline until it could find providers willing to work with the app.

This is an example of how nongovernment entities (such as corporations) can play a role in protecting or limiting free speech. It is important to note that while "Congress shall make no law" restricting the people's right to speech, private organizations, communities, and platforms may create their own rules with regard to what is appropriate or permitted within their own context.

CHAPTER 3

Comparing Countries Around the World

The United States is considered an outlier when it comes to freedom of expression. No other country, democracy or otherwise, goes as far as the United States to protect all kinds of speech, even speech that's deemed offensive. Other democracies emphasize a balance between freedom of expression and other values such as safety, dignity, or the communal good. The United States, in contrast, often views freedom of speech as superior to other rights.

Comparing the United States and Europe

According to an analysis by legal scholars in 2016, the United States and Europe are more similar than different when it comes to freedom of speech. Article 10 of the European

Opposite: In Paris, France, protesters wear yellow vests and gather to protest the high cost of living, high taxes, and high fuel costs in their country. Article 10 of the European Convention protects their right to protest.

Convention on Human Rights, written in 1950, is similar in concept to the First Amendment to the US Constitution. Article 10 states:

1. *Everyone has the right to freedom of expression. This right shall include freedom to hold opinions and to receive and impart information and ideas without interference by public authority and regardless of frontiers. This Article shall not prevent [European countries] from requiring the licensing of broadcasting, television, or cinema enterprises.*

2. *The exercise of these freedoms, since it carries with it duties and responsibilities, may be subject to such formalities, conditions, restrictions, or penalties as are prescribed by law and are necessary in a democratic society, in the interests of national security, territorial integrity or public safety, for the prevention of disorder or crime, for the protection of health or morals, for the protection of the reputation or rights of others, for preventing the disclosure of information received in confidence, or for maintaining the authority and impartiality of the judiciary.*

One significant difference between the First Amendment (United States) and Article 10 (for Europe) is that the European model frames the right to speak as a positive ("Everyone has the right to speak.") rather than a negative ("Congress shall make no law [restricting freedom of speech]."). The second significant difference is that Article 10 lays out clear limitations for when freedom of speech may be restricted, while the United States has relied on

On November 4, 1950, many European leaders gathered together to sign the European Convention on Human Rights.

nearly a century of interpretation through the Supreme Court to map the boundaries of speech.

In addition to the language of the documents themselves, there are two ways in which interpretations of freedom of speech in the United States have differed substantially from interpretations in Europe and elsewhere. One difference relates to commercial speech (advertising). The United States Supreme Court has given less consistent rulings about commercial speech than Europe, taking a case-by-case approach. Also, commercial speech in the United States is more likely to be protected when it is in the best interest of consumers. In contrast, the European Court has tried to balance the interests of both the speaker and audience. Europe also emphasizes the watchdog role of news media more than the United States does when deciding how much authority to give states in regulating media. Another difference between the United States and Europe has to do with the degree of tolerance allowed for hate and extremist speech. Perhaps because of the historical events of the Holocaust, European countries are much less tolerant of hate and extremist speech.

Comparing Laws Against Hate Speech

The American Library Association states that there isn't a legal definition for hate speech in the United States, but in general, it is "any form of expression through which speakers intend to vilify, humiliate, or incite hatred against a group or a class of persons." Hate speech is protected in the United States unless it incites imminent law-breaking or specific threats of violence targeted at a person or group.

As the Supreme Court ruling in *Matal v. Tam* (2017) states, "Speech that demeans on the basis of race, ethnicity, gender, religion, age, disability, or any other similar ground is hateful; but the proudest boast of our free speech jurisprudence is that we protect the freedom to express 'the thought that we hate.'"

On March 31, 2007, members of Union Bell Baptist Church in Stafford, Virginia, cleaned up vandalism that included racial and religious slurs.

Hate speech is protected in the United States, but hate crimes are not. Property damage, violation of civil rights, and acts of intimidation are punishable as hate crimes. As previously mentioned, the FBI has set a definition for hate crimes: "criminal offense against a person or property motivated in whole or in part by an offender's

Commercial Speech

In Canada, as in the United States, large warning labels are placed on cigarette packages. This is a type of enforced commercial speech because the government requires the companies to add the text to the product.

Commercial speech includes advertising for products and services. It also includes political speech. Commercial speech is a special category that was not protected in the United States until 1976 when the Supreme Court held that commercial speech (such as advertising) fit under the umbrella of First Amendment rights. The reasoning was that such information could benefit consumers in their decision making. In this case, the rights of the audience (consumers, customers, and clients) was considered as important as the rights of the advertiser. Protections for commercial speech have expanded over time through court decisions. They now allow greater freedom in what can be advertised.

In 1985, the Supreme Court ruled that not only could commercial speech be protected, it could also be required in certain cases. This was called "compelled commercial speech" and includes nutrition labels on foods, warning labels on cigarettes, and the requirement that ads from lawyers include a statement that their clients might be liable to pay legal fees. The purpose of this compelled commercial speech is to inform people and to prevent companies from misleading the public.

Commercial speech is now protected in both the United States and in Europe, but both regions are still struggling to find the balance between consumer interests and the interests of commercial speakers (corporations).

bias against a race, religion, disability, sexual orientation, ethnicity, gender, or gender identity." Democracies other than the United States, however, have followed a different path. In many European countries, South Africa, and elsewhere, specific laws restrict hate speech even if it does not lead to physical violence.

Laws Against Hate Speech in Other Democracies

Legal scholar Jean-Marie Kamatali writes about the differences between American views on protections for hate and extremist speech and views from Europe, Canada, and other democracies. Kamatali's article "The Limits of the First Amendment: Protecting American Citizens' Free Speech in the Era of the Internet and the Global Marketplace of Ideas" points out that many free and democratic countries such as Canada, Denmark, France, Germany, South Africa, and others have laws to punish hate and extremist speech. For example, Canada has several laws to prohibit hate speech, including the Criminal Code, Canadian Human Rights Act, and additional human rights legislation specific to each province. Speech that promotes genocide, or that incites hatred against a particular group, is punishable by Canadian law. According to the Supreme Court of Canada, hate speech causes "real harm" to the victim and to society. This contrasts with American view of hate and extremist speech, which justifies such speech based on the "marketplace of ideas," "self-governance," and "tolerant society." Canadian Supreme Court Chief Justice Dickson says that "there is very little chance that statements intended to promote hatred against an identifiable group are true, or that their vision of society will lead to a better world."

Germany enforces strict laws about displaying Nazi symbols and uniforms. This Nazi uniform is displayed in a museum, which is allowed by German law so that people can learn from the past.

France has laws that punish public speech and images that encourage hatred or discrimination based on ethnicity, nationality, or religion. It is also illegal in France to deny the Holocaust and to wear or display uniforms or emblems related to people or groups that committed crimes against humanity (such as the Nazi swastika, for example). French criminal law includes limits for hate speech on websites that can be accessed in France, even if that content was posted in a different country, such as the United States.

Kamatali explains that in Germany, "four categories of speech are criminalized: 1) that which incites hatred against segments of the population, 2) that which assaults the human dignity of others, 3) that which produces hate speech, 4) that which publicly denies the Holocaust." Interestingly, the German Federal Court of Justice ruled that these laws apply also to foreigners who post extremist and hate speech on the internet. This means that American citizens who violate German laws (while still remaining within the bounds of First Amendment rights) could be prosecuted in Germany.

To many people, it is understandable why such laws were deemed necessary. The people of Germany, France, and elsewhere were traumatized by the Holocaust and World War II. Kamatali explains, "As a result, they were more willing to give up some of their rights to speak in order to ensure that the types of speech and writing that led to concentration camps and genocide would not happen again. What is less clear is what happens when outsiders post speech on the World Wide Web that violates European laws."

The United Kingdom has laws regarding hate speech that are similar to those in Canada, Germany, and France. For example, "A person who uses threatening, abusive, or insulting words or behavior" is guilty of breaking the law if "he intends to stir up racial hatred." This is quite different from the US Supreme Court's ruling in the Brandenburg case, which asks for evidence that the speech not only intends to stir up violence, but is likely to result in real physical harm.

When American Hate Speech Is Transmitted Abroad

The difference in attitude toward hate and extremist speech between the United States and other countries has led to some interesting situations for Americans when traveling abroad. An American

Thanks to the internet, messages are quickly and easily transmitted beyond national boundaries. This means messages permitted in one country can be sent into countries where they are forbidden.

citizen whose words reach one of the above countries (via hate speech posted online, for example) can be prosecuted in the other country. Although an American will not be arrested on US soil for laws they have violated in other countries, they could risk arrest when traveling to those countries.

In May 2010, American law professor Peter Erlinder was arrested in Rwanda for presentations he had made in the United States that violated a Rwandan law about genocide denial. In another example, in 2001, two French nonprofit organizations sued the American company Yahoo! because its online auction site included Nazi memorabilia, and French law forbade French citizens from having access to such items. The district court ruled in favor of Yahoo!, but the French organizations appealed to a higher court. Eventually, in 2006, the case reached the United States Supreme Court, which refused to hear the case against Yahoo! The question was whether the First Amendment rights of Americans still apply when they reach outside US borders and conflict with other nations' laws—and that question has not yet been fully answered.

These are just a few examples of how different views of freedom of speech between the United States and other nations have sparked controversy and created difficulty in applying international law.

David Kaye and the United Nations

Starting in 1993, the United Nations began to regularly appoint someone to promote and protect the "right to freedom of opinion and expression" worldwide. The title of this job is "UN Special Rapporteur on the promotion and protection of the right to freedom of opinion and expression." David Kaye was appointed to this job in August 2014. He must gather facts and information about any violations of the right to freedom of opinion and expression.

David Kaye of the United Nations advocates for freedom of speech for people around the world.

As part of his work in this role, David Kaye and his team have reported on the problem of weak data encryption. Encryption allows internet users to remain anonymous while they search the web and access information online. Weak encryption means that people may think their privacy is being protected when they are online while it actually is not. This can be an especially bad problem for people in countries with government surveillance or government hacking. Weak encryption is problematic for anyone who wants sensitive information to remain private, such as credit card and banking information or health data.

The report by Kaye and his team discussed the role of corporations in protecting freedom of expression. It states that companies that support messaging apps, like WeChat, WhatsApp, and Viber, play a critical role in supporting free expression.

CHAPTER 4

The Power of the People

G ains in civil rights for women, for African Americans, for LGBTQ+ community members, and for people with disabilities have all come about in part because of the freedom of speech, including the right to peacefully protest and peacefully demonstrate.

For example, American women worked for decades to express their desire to vote and own property in the United States. They used speeches, letters, books, pamphlets, and protests to ask the government to change the voting laws.

The Civil Rights Act of 1965 came into being because of thousands of men and women, young and old, who spent decades protesting the unfair and discriminatory laws and practices in the United States. The Reverend Dr. Martin Luther King Jr., Rosa Parks, and others used nonviolent demonstrations and protests to demand change. Today, virtually everyone in American society benefits from greater equality and justice.

Opposite: On March 24, 2018, hundreds of thousands of people gathered in Washington, DC, during the March for Our Lives to rally support for new gun safety laws.

People celebrate in New York City on June 26, 2015, the day the Supreme Court ruled that same-sex marriages are valid across the United States.

Members of the LGBTQ+ community and their allies worked tirelessly during the 1980s, 1990s, and the early 2000s to ask for equal rights to access medical care, to marry and have children, and to be treated fairly in the workplace. Their marches, letters, and other activism led to New York State's Marriage Equality Act of 2011. The act allowed for legal marriages between same-sex couples while preventing states and other institutions from making those marriages illegitimate. In 2015, the Supreme Court of the United States ruled in *Obergefell v. Hodges* that same-sex marriages were legal in all fifty states.

Historically, young people have often been the ones to show up for sit-ins and protests. Perhaps this is because young people have the most at stake. This motivates them to demand social change. Today, the means by which young people can express their opinions have expanded to include online formats such as memes, Twitter, blogs, and other social media platforms. But traditional forms of expression remain important to accomplishing new goals.

Today's Protests

Currently, activists continue to tackle issues from previous generations while working toward change on new issues too. Gun laws, climate change, racial bias, and economic inequity are a few of the up-and-coming themes of recent protests in the United States and in other countries. These protests show the freedom of speech in action.

The National Anthem Protests

In 2016, during pre-season, NFL player Colin Kaepernick chose to protest something he saw as a social problem. Many African American men had been killed by police officers and those officers were never charged or punished. Kaepernick decided to express himself by sitting or kneeling during the playing of the National Anthem instead of standing. It was a silent and nonviolent protest. Kaepernick said, "I am not going to stand up to show pride in a flag for a country that oppresses black people and people of color. To me, this is bigger than football, and it would be selfish on my part to look the other way. There are bodies in the street and people getting paid leave and getting away with murder." Soon, other athletes joined him by sitting or kneeling during the anthem. Over the next two years, about two hundred NFL players participated. Athletes in other sports, such as professional soccer player Megan Rapinoe, joined. Some high school athletes have also knelt or sat to protest police brutality.

This action has affected Colin Kaepernick's football career. His contract with the San Francisco 49ers expired at the end of the 2016 season, and he was not hired by another NFL team afterward. In 2018, Nike aired an ad featuring Kaepernick saying, "Believe in something. Even if it means sacrificing everything."

While many Americans have viewed the NFL athletes' speech as being protected under federal law, others have pointed out that the NFL is their employer. As previously discussed, employees in the workplace are subject to restrictions their employer places on them. The controversy over NFL players "taking a knee" in protest while on the playing field has raised interesting and compelling arguments about the value and appropriate limits of free speech. For example, some people have expressed support for the players' right to protest, even though they did not necessarily agree with the particular form of protest. Others have agreed with the message, but not the time or place. Still others believe that the protest has been successful precisely because of how it got an important conversation going

In the fall of 2016, NFL quarterback Colin Kaepernick chose to sit during the National Anthem before a game to protest racial injustice. He switched his protest mode from sitting to kneeling after a military veteran suggested this would be more respectful.

among a broader section of the American public. Different media sources represented the protests differently, with some viewing it as disrespectful to the military and nation, and others viewing it as a legitimate form of free expression and a way to raise attention to social justice issues.

Women's Rights Protests

The largest one-day protest in American history took place the day after President Donald Trump's inauguration. The Women's March brought together people from many different backgrounds and beliefs. Women old and young, men, and children gathered together in Washington, DC. Many wore hand-knit pink hats with cat ears that represented feminism.

Marchers represented a wide range of perspectives, such as groups supporting immigrants, groups wishing to resist laws that limited the rights of women, and many others. Despite the large numbers, the protest remained peaceful.

Expressing Free Speech in Favor of Science and Addressing Climate Change

As the effects of global climate change have started to impact communities and individuals, people have taken action to demand that their governments be more proactive in taking steps to reduce harm. Around the world, numerous protests have asked leaders to change economic and social policies and practices. Scientists have raised alarms about the negative impact on people, animals, and the environment that rising levels of carbon dioxide and methane are having. Many citizens believe that politicians have not responded as strongly and productively as they should have. Protests in the United States and Paris in 2018 are just a couple of examples. These

Record-Breaking Protests in 2017 and 2018

The four largest protests in American history took place in 2017 and 2018.

The 2017 Women's March on Washington (and sister marches) broke records for all previous protests in US history with an estimated 4.2 million to 5.2 million people in attendance. One year later, the 2018 Women's March was the second largest protest in US history with 1.5 million marchers. The third largest protest was March for Our Lives, which took place on March 24, 2018, with 1.2 million to 2 million attendees. The March for Science (April 22, 2017) included an estimated 1 million participants.

Frustrated with the large number of protests, President Donald Trump has criticized the rights of protesters. In October 2018, the American Civil Liberties Union reported that the Trump administration proposed to "dramatically limit the right to demonstrate near the White House and on the National Mall in ways that would violate court orders that have stood for decades." The Trump administration also proposes charging expensive fees to discourage protesters. This proposal raises questions about First Amendment rights including the freedom of assembly, the freedom of speech, and the right to petition one's government.

Some United Nations experts have expressed concern about many state-level proposals to criminalize peaceful protests as well as militant, violent responses to protests such as the response to Native Americans who opposed the Dakota Access Pipeline, an oil pipeline that cuts through sacred lands. The responses of the UN, the Trump administration, and the ACLU show the complexity of First Amendment rights and the ways that interpretations shift over time.

In 2017, the Standing Rock Tribe and many supporters protested the construction of the Dakota Access Pipeline, which now runs through sacred lands.

Pink hats with cat ears became a symbol for women's rights in the days surrounding President Trump's inauguration and were featured in the 2017 Women's March and again in the 2018 Women's March.

protests related to several First Amendment protections, including the right to petition the government to address grievances.

March for Our Lives

On February 14, 2018, a gunman killed seventeen people at Marjory Stoneman Douglas High School in Parkland, Florida. Seventeen others were injured. It was the deadliest mass shooting in an American high school. Survivors from the school, including Emma Gonzalez and David Hogg, organized a movement called Never Again MSD to raise the age for buying guns in Florida from eighteen to twenty-one and to ask for other improvements in gun regulations. Soon after, the Marjory Stoneman Douglas High School Public Safety Act was passed in Florida. It made several changes to Florida law to help reduce the chance of a similar violent attack occurring in the future. On March 24, 2018, the March for Our Lives was held in Washington, DC, while other demonstrations took place throughout the United States. This protest is an example of young people—even those too young to vote—participating in democracy. They peaceably expressed themselves through speech and by gathering in assembly. Although the movement has not had a significant effect at the federal level, it has helped bring about substantial changes at the state level.

Apart from legislation, public opinion caused stores like Dick's Sporting Goods and Walmart to increase the age requirement for gun purchases to twenty-one. Discussions around the country continue to focus on how to improve school safety.

The Dilemma of Free Speech and Expression

Each generation has the privilege and responsibility of re-interpreting democracy for its current situation. The Founding Fathers expected that democracy would be an evolving form of government that responded to the changing needs of the people. Today's society is very different from life in the 1790s, and even our methods for expressing ourselves have changed dramatically. The writers of the Constitution could not have imagined the internet and how quickly ideas could be shared and spread.

For more than two centuries of American history, the Constitution has been amended and the courts have interpreted it—sometimes

Emma Gonzalez, from Marjory Stoneman Douglas High School in Parkland, Florida, has become a fierce advocate for changes to gun laws. She helped to organize Never Again MSD, which led to the March for Our Lives protest.

increasing freedom of expression and sometimes limiting it. The First Amendment has retained its importance, but the work of applying it is never done. First Amendment rights must be balanced with the other important values of a democracy, such as the equality of all people, and the protection of others' rights and safety. This is the dilemma that comes along with freedom of speech. No freedom is absolute. Every freedom—including the freedom of speech and of expression—must be limited to some extent in the interest of balance. Society is always weighing the good of the individual against the good of the group. Often, what is good for one is good for the whole, such as when citizens peacefully share their ideas and beliefs through their words, actions, and in writing. However, when someone's words lead to harm or violence, then discussion about appropriate limitations is warranted.

The word dilemma means "two horns." One horn in this dilemma is the freedom of expression guaranteed in the First Amendment and the valid concern about having these rights restricted unnecessarily. The other horn is the desire to protect the rights of others and the concern that some speech and expression, particularly intolerant or hate speech, can cause harm to others. Every discussion of free speech must keep an eye out for both horns to avoid the consequences of landing on one sharp horn or the other.

Staying Informed

Keeping up with the news is the best way to understand how interpretations of the freedom of speech change over time.

For a deeper level of engagement, you can follow organizations that work to protect people's rights. Some well-established organizations that work on freedom of speech are the Anti-Defamation League, the American Civil Liberties Union (ACLU), National Association for the Advancement of Colored People (NAACP), the Southern Poverty Law Center, Human Rights Watch, and the United Nations Human Rights Committee.

Always check the credibility of each organization you encounter. One way is to read the reviews of the organization on the website Charity Navigator. Look for organizations that are transparent, honest, open, and ethical with their funds, and are generally well-respected. Avoid groups that are overly secretive or that tend toward violence.

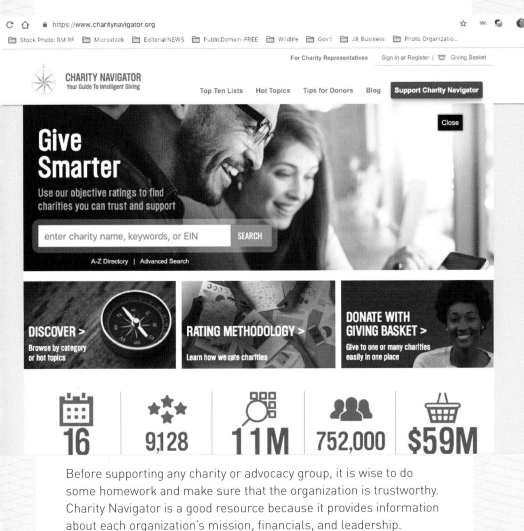

Before supporting any charity or advocacy group, it is wise to do some homework and make sure that the organization is trustworthy. Charity Navigator is a good resource because it provides information about each organization's mission, financials, and leadership.

GLOSSARY

amendments Updates to an existing document.

autonomy The freedom to make decisions on one's own.

Bill of Rights The first ten amendments to the US Constitution, which were written to ensure certain freedoms for American citizens.

defamation Speech (written and verbal) that is untrue and that intentionally causes harm to another person's reputation, and which may be punishable.

democracy A form of government in which leaders are freely elected by the people whom they will represent and govern.

Enlightenment A movement during the eighteenth century that valued reason and science over superstition. Also called the "Age of Reason," its ideas influenced the American colonists who founded the United States.

genocide An attempt to kill or remove an entire population or group of people.

justification An argument or reason in support of something.

libel To write false statements about a person's character in order to damage his or her reputation.

marketplace of ideas The notion developed by Supreme Court justice Oliver Wendell Holmes that all ideas, even bad ones, should be shared freely in order to allow people to be able to choose the best ones.

paradox When two opposite and contradictory ideas seem to be equally true.

slander To verbally make false statements about a person's character in order to damage his or her reputation.

social contract The idea that all people in a society willingly give up some of their autonomy in order to receive benefits, such as safety and protection, from the group.

suppress To hold back or push down.

tolerance Willingness to allow points of view or actions with which one does not agree.

user agreement A document that lays out the terms under which a person may use a social media platform, application, software, or other services. A user who violates the terms may be warned or banned from using the services.

FURTHER INFORMATION

Books

Doyle, Eamon. *Freedom of Speech on Campus*. New York: Greenhaven, 2018.

Gold, Susan Dudley. *Protecting Hate Speech: R. A. V. v. St. Paul*. First Amendment Cases. New York: Cavendish Square, 2014.

Rauf, Don. *Everything You Need to Know About Free Speech*. New York: Rosen Publishing, 2018.

Websites

First Amendment Quiz

https://splc.org/first-amendment-quiz

Take an interactive quiz about the First Amendment created by the Student Press Law Center.

Free Speech

https://www.aclu.org/issues/free-speech

Find up-to-the-minute reporting, a timeline, and more on the ACLU's website.

Interactive Constitution

https://constitutioncenter.org/interactive-constitution#

Explore the Constitution and read articles that provide historical context and explanations of key court cases.

Videos

Freedom of Speech: Crash Course Government and Politics #25

https://www.youtube.com/watch?v=Zeeq0qaEaLw

Learn more about the limits of free speech
in this entertaining video.

What Does "Freedom of Speech" Mean in the US?

https://www.youtube.com/watch?v=NL93bGkDOZE

The History Channel traces the freedom of speech
from its origins through some of the most important
court cases of the twentieth century.

BIBLIOGRAPHY

Berman, Micah L. "Clarifying Standards for Compelled Commercial Speech." *Wash. U. Journal of Law & Policy* 50, no. 3 (2016). http://openscholarship.wustl.edu/law_journal_law_policy/vol50/iss1/3.

FindLaw. "Freedom of Speech in the Workplace: The First Amendment Revisited." Accessed on December 1, 2018. https://corporate.findlaw.com/law-library/freedom-of-speech-in-the-workplace-the-first-amendment-revisited.html.

Gordon, Gregory S. "Hate Speech and Persecution: A Contextual Approach." *Vanderbilt Journal of Transnational Law* 46, no. 2 (March 2013): 303–73. http://search.ebscohost.com/login.aspx?direct=true&AuthType=cookie,ip,cpid,athens,shib&custid=s8863137&db=a9h&AN=87367955&site=ehost-live&scope=site&custid=s8863137.

Johnson, Bruce E. H., and Kyu Ho Youm. "Commercial Speech and Free Expression: The United States and Europe Compared." *Journal of International Entertainment & Media Law* 2, no. 2 (Winter 2009): 159–198.

Kamatali, Jean-Marie. "The Limits of the First Amendment: Protecting American Citizens' Free Speech in the Era of the Internet and the Global Marketplace of Ideas." *Wisconsin International Law Journal* 33, no. 4 (March 1, 2016).

Legal Information Institute. "Obscenity." Accessed on December 1, 2018. https://www.law.cornell.edu/wex/obscenity.

National School Boards Association. "Coercion, Conscience, and the First Amendment: A Legal Guide for Public Schools on the Regulation of Student and Employee Speech." January 2018. https://cdn-files.nsba.org/s3fs-public/reports/First_Amendment_Guide-2018.pdf?KgOvuu2Dp8KvWkiwF_I9hHhv4wsUROez.

Roose, Kevin. "On Gab, an Extremist-Friendly Site, Pittsburgh Shooting Suspect Aired His Hatred in Full." *New York Times*, October 28, 2018.

Rosenfeld, Michael. "Review: Extremist Speech and the Paradox of Tolerance." *Harvard Law Review* 100, no. 6 (April 1987): 1457–1481.

Sherman, Michael J. "Brandenburg v. Twitter." *George Mason University Civil Rights Law Journal* 28, no. 2 (March 1, 2018): 127–172.

United States Courts. "What Does Free Speech Mean?" Accessed on December 1, 2018. http://www.uscourts.gov/about-federal-courts/educational-resources/about-educational-outreach/activity-resources/what-does.

US Department of Justice. "Citizen's Guide to U. S. Federal Law on Obscenity." Accessed on December 1, 2018. https://www.justice.gov/criminal-ceos/citizens-guide-us-federal-law-obscenity.

Weinberger, Matt, and Steve Kovach. "The Google Employee Who Wrote the Controversial Google Manifesto Was Fired After CEO Sundar Pichai Called It 'Not OK.'" *Business Insider*, August 7, 2017. https://www.businessinsider.com/google-sundar-pichai-anti-diversity-manifesto-fired-2017-8.

INDEX

Page numbers in **boldface** refer to images.

ABOUT THE AUTHOR

Anna Maria Johnson teaches courses about writing and the humanities at James Madison University in the School of Writing, Rhetoric, and Technical Communication. She specializes in critical reading, critical thinking, information literacy, research skills, and personal essays. Johnson holds an MFA in Writing from Vermont College of Fine Arts. She lives in the Shenandoah Valley, about two hours from Washington, DC, with photographer Steven David Johnson, their two daughters, one dog, and three to five cats.